LETTING GO
OF ANXIETY

Alison Perkins

Amazon Publishing

Book design by Rachel Perkins

ISBN: 9798725739275 (paperback)

Dedicated to Joshua Perkins,
who is a constant encouragement
and source of wisdom.

And to our beloved friends in Bahrain,
whose loving kindness has been a blessing
to us for the past 15 years.

.

PRELUDE

WHAT'S THERE TO BE ANXIOUS ABOUT?

This devotional is written in the year 2020. I don't know what the future will hold, but 2020 has been a year full of anxiety. In January we held our breath watching the United States and Iran walk right up to the line of military confrontation before slowly backing away. February brought the first global ripples of the coronavirus. By March those ripples turned into a global tsunami that crashed onto every nation's shores, forcing closures and lockdowns worldwide. June brought protests about racial injustice in the United States that continued to simmer for months. Those protests reverberated around the world, spurring protests in support of racial justice in the U.S., or addressing racial injustice in their own communities. Some protests have been peaceful, some have not. In addition, 2020 contained one of the most divisive U.S. presidential elections in recent memory. Each of those global events have myriad implications for a host of individuals' health, jobs, savings, education, and daily living. It was a very stressful year.

I work as a principal of a school in the Arabian Peninsula, and in March of 2020 we were forced to transition from on-campus learning to online learning overnight when the government closed all schools. The situation would change on a weekly, daily, and sometimes hourly basis. Students, including my own children, did work from home as educators tried to figure out how best to meet the needs of students without burning out from the volume of work and stress of doing things in ways we had never known before. Even now, we wrestle at school with how best to educate kids and balance good education practice, the limits of education, the needs of different families in our school, and how much can actually be achieved by our community.

Like many people around the world, physically gathering with our church community has been sporadic at best. While we are thankful that we can have church online and meet with our small group via Zoom, it is not the same as the physical gathering of the saints to pray and worship corporately, to enjoy encouragement and exhortation through the preaching of the word, and to participate in communion as a family of believers.

All of this is on top of the normal stresses people experience: marital issues, work stress, financial worries, concerns about children, and all the other normal anxieties that press on us from one day to the next.

Anxiety is a relevant topic.

Yet Peter exhorts his readers saying, "*Don't be anxious.*" My initial reaction is to roll my eyes. Is it realistic to not be anxious in 2020? Did Peter ever try leading a school in a global pandemic, where everyone has different family situations, technology, and desires for education? Did he ever have to wonder whether his private school would financially survive? What problems did Peter face that could ever measure up to the problems we are facing today?

But when I go back and read the entirety of Peter's first letter, I see him writing to a church community that strikes me as familiar:

- There is a call to be holy, and to put off the sin in our lives, and to abstain from the passions of the flesh. *In Rome, a city of pagan passions.*

- There is a call to submit to the governing authorities— and he doesn't distinguish between good governing authorities and bad ones. *In Rome, where the governing authorities despised the Church's religious convictions.*

- There is a call for healthy and loving family relationships between husbands and wives. *In Rome, where men ruled over women, and women were treated more like property than like partners.*

- He calls for long-suffering in the face of persecution. *In Rome, where Christians were persecuted to their deaths for their faith.*

- Lastly, he calls on the church elders to be humble, grace-filled, and loving leaders to their congregation.

In the first century, where the elders and church leaders were leading a church and being a part of church for the very first time.

I can imagine the early churches reading Peter's letter and thinking, "Good grief. Is he serious? We're supposed to do all that?" It's almost as if Peter never even led a church!

Or maybe he did. And maybe that's why the Holy Spirit inspired him to wrap up his letter discussing anxiety.

At the beginning of the book of 1 Peter, he reminds his readers of a future held for them by God. Therefore, it is with confidence he admonishes the early church (as well as the survivors of 2020) to "cast all our anxieties on Him, for he cares for us." It is a future where the saints persevere, holding fast to God the Father through faith in Christ Jesus, in the power of the Holy Spirit. Let's go back and read 1 Peter 1:3-7:

> *[3b]According to his great mercy, he has caused us to be born again to a living hope through the resurrection of Jesus Christ from the dead, [4]to an inheritance that is imperishable,* undefiled, and unfading, kept in heaven for you, *[5]who by God's power are being guarded through faith for a salvation ready to be revealed in the last time. [6]In this you rejoice, though now for a little while, if necessary, you have been grieved by various trials, [7]so that the tested genuineness of your faith—* more precious than gold *that perishes though it is tested by fire—may be found to result in praise and glory and honor at the revelation of Jesus Christ. (emphasis added)*

In addressing anxiety, Peter also reminds us of what our future holds for us in the first place. Addressing anxiety isn't some mystical practice of removing negative thoughts from our minds. It is the active replacement of those negative thoughts with a vision of the risen Lord, and the inheritance that is kept for us.

Therefore, when reading this devotional and participating in this study, don't just read it to calm your anxieties. Read it to feast on the goodness of God. Remember, brothers and sisters, you are being guarded through faith for a salvation ready to be revealed in the last time.

JOSH PERKINS
Husband of Alison, 2020

INTRODUCTION

ANXIETY IS ONE OF those things that can be hard to avoid, at least while one is still breathing. Every soul has seasons of life with greater and lesser amounts of stress, worries, concerns, and cares. God encourages us to think about and plan for the future, however, He explicitly commanded us not to be anxious or to worry. A wise man prepares and plans for the future. An anxious man excessively worries about situations over which he has no control. A wise man may purchase life insurance, while an anxious man will stay up all night worrying how his family will cope should he die unexpectedly. A wise man has regular visits to the doctor; an anxious man may avoid annual checkups for fear of bad news of ailing health. Wisdom is reasonable preparedness. Anxiety is worrying over endless possibilities of bad scenarios.

Anxiety is not necessarily caused by stress, but the two can go hand in hand. Stressful situations can often push us past our prepared resources and reserves, leaving us to either hope in the Lord's promised provisions, or worry. All people will have to deal with stressful situations and seasons in their lives, because this is a fallen world filled with thorns and thistles. In coming through those situations however, I believe the Lord wants us to learn to trust in his goodness. In general, we don't have a lot of control over the stresses of our lives, but we do have control over our anxieties and worries. How then can we deal with stress and anxiety in a Christ-honoring way? I believe the Word has given us great tools to actively work against anxiety and worry that are complex, comprehensive, and doable.

For this study, we will be looking deeply at 1 Peter 5:6-7:

[6]"Humble yourselves, therefore, under the mighty hand of God so that at the proper time he may exalt you, [7]casting all your anxieties on him, because he cares for you."

We will explore each phrase of this verse and apply it to our anxieties and worries. We will also study additional texts to highlight how effectively this verse can bring peace to our souls.

COMMON WORRIES VERSUS ANXIETY DISORDERS

The purpose of this study is to give good nourishing food for the mind and soul, strengthening it to deal with the fears and apprehensions that come with life's inherent stress. However, it bears noting that this is not the same as combating the more complex spectrum of anxiety disorders. This study is not meant to replace God-given therapy or medication for those who suffer from such challenges. It is meant to highlight how the Gospel can strengthen our souls to aid us in dealing with life's stressful situations. Everybody needs a general supply of life-sustaining vitamins and minerals, however, no doctor would suggest combating cancer by only increasing your intake of broccoli each week. The mind is a complex organ, and God has given equally complex and diverse therapies and medicines for some of its ailments, such as anxiety disorders. I hope that everyone struggling with anxiety can find useful tools from this study, but for those brothers and sisters whose struggle is more profound, I sincerely hope they feel the freedom to reach out for more comprehensive therapies.

WAYS TO USE THIS BOOK

This was originally written as a topical Bible study on anxiety to be done within a church small group. I have written a devotional for each week, but kept the original small group structure at the end of each chapter with questions for discussion. However, even without a small group you are welcome to go through the questions as a personal devotion.

Chapter One

HUMILITY

Humble yourselves, therefore, *under the mighty hand of God so that at the proper time he may exalt you, casting all your anxieties on him, because he cares for you.*

1 Peter 5:6-7

1 PETER IS FULL of commands on how to conduct our lives. We are to live holy lives. We are to submit to governing authorities. We are to love our spouses and our children. We are to persevere in the midst of persecution. Church leaders are commanded to

remain humble and loving, while trying to lead people through all the messy problems within their communities. Most people might have anxiety just from the sheer weight of these expectations. It is impossible. It is humbling. And it is with humility that Peter starts his address on anxiety. We can't get God's help with anxiety without first admitting that we need his help. Humility admits that we cannot do it on our own, and admits we need someone else's help. Humility acknowledges our own weaknesses. It is the opposite of thinking we are our own savior and our own god.

But how exactly do we humble ourselves? What practical steps can we take towards becoming more humble? Sometimes, in order to gain insight into what does work, it's helpful to look at what doesn't work. Isaiah 58:1–59:2 illustrates how people attempted humility while still hoping to be their own savior, resulting in God's judgment and scorn. They thought they were approaching God with reverence, but according to his rebuke, they had completely failed. While this text may be highlighting some failures we can avoid, it also shows four powerful and practical ways to humble ourselves before the Lord.

Read with me Isaiah 58:1–59:2.

> 58:1 *"Cry aloud; do not hold back;*
>   *lift up your voice like a trumpet;*
> *declare to my people their transgression,*
>   *to the house of Jacob their sins.*
> *2Yet they seek me daily*
>   *and delight to know my ways,*
> *as if they were a nation that did righteousness*
>   *and did not forsake the judgment of their God;*
> *they ask of me righteous judgments;*
>   *they delight to draw near to God.*
> *3'Why have we fasted, and you see it not?*

Why have we humbled ourselves, and you take no
knowledge of it?'
Behold, in the day of your fast you seek your own pleasure,
and oppress all your workers.
⁴Behold, you fast only to quarrel and to fight
and to hit with a wicked fist.
Fasting like yours this day
will not make your voice to be heard on high.
⁵Is such the fast that I choose,
a day for a person to humble himself?
Is it to bow down his head like a reed,
and to spread sackcloth and ashes under him?
Will you call this a fast,
and a day acceptable to the LORD?

⁶"Is not this the fast that I choose:
to loose the bonds of wickedness,
to undo the straps of the yoke,
to let the oppressed go free,
and to break every yoke?
⁷Is it not to share your bread with the hungry
and bring the homeless poor into your house;
when you see the naked, to cover him,
and not to hide yourself from your own flesh?
⁸Then shall your light break forth like the dawn,
and your healing shall spring up speedily;
your righteousness shall go before you;
the glory of the LORD shall be your rear guard.
⁹Then you shall call, and the LORD will answer;
you shall cry, and he will say, 'Here I am.'
If you take away the yoke from your midst,
the pointing of the finger, and speaking wickedness,
¹⁰if you pour yourself out for the hungry
and satisfy the desire of the afflicted,

then shall your light rise in the darkness
and your gloom be as the noonday.
11And the LORD will guide you continually
and satisfy your desire in scorched places
and make your bones strong;
and you shall be like a watered garden,
like a spring of water,
whose waters do not fail.
12And your ancient ruins shall be rebuilt;
you shall raise up the foundations of many generations;
you shall be called the repairer of the breach,
the restorer of streets to dwell in.

13"If you turn back your foot from the Sabbath,
from doing your pleasure on my holy day,
and call the Sabbath a delight
and the holy day of the LORD honorable;
if you honor it, not going your own ways,
or seeking your own pleasure, or talking idly;
14then you shall take delight in the LORD,
and I will make you ride on the heights of the earth;
I will feed you with the heritage of Jacob your father,
for the mouth of the LORD has spoken."

59:1Behold, the LORD's hand is not shortened, that it
cannot save,
or his ear dull, that it cannot hear;
2but your iniquities have made a separation
between you and your God,
and your sins have hidden his face from you
so that he does not hear.

These people are my kind of people. They were raised religious, they acted religious, and they even dressed religious. As someone who has been around religion my whole life, I can identify with the Israelites. Looking at their lives is like looking into a mirror. I know it very well could be me sitting under God's judgment for putting hope in my own self-righteousness. Verses 1 & 2 show that their religiosity only served to gratify themselves, a far cry from James' description of true religion that stretches past oneself into caring for widows and orphans (James 1:27).

FASTING

> [3]'Why have we fasted, and you see it not?
>   Why have we humbled ourselves, and you take no
>   knowledge of it?'
> Behold, in the day of your fast you seek your own pleasure,
>   and oppress all your workers.

In verse 3 we see the Israelites' frustration with God. Maybe you can identify with them because your attempts at serving God seem to go completely unnoticed? They thought their fasts were acts of humility and righteousness—a way to turn God's head. Yet for all their work, God remained silent. Their prayers were falling on deaf ears in heaven.

They were not wrong to think of fasting as a way to humble themselves. In verse 6, God clearly calls his people to humble themselves with fasting. However, it is much more than just the physical act of not eating. Throughout scripture, fasting is a prac-tical and physical way to draw near to God. God's people fast in order to repent, while they are mourning, to make a petition, and to simply hear His voice. It is the physical expression of John the Bap-tist's worship of the Christ when he extolled, "He must increase, but I must decrease" (John 3:30).

Fasting helps us remember that we are ultimately dependent

on the Lord for our sustenance, and that our spiritual nourishment from Him is more important than our daily bread. It is a powerful acknowledgment of our position before God, that he is our ultimate sustainer. Fasting is a physical posture of humility.

How can fasting help us deal with anxiety? I have found that fasting brings relief from worries that are outside of my control. During my Christian walk, there have been many heartbreaking situations that I simply do not know how to solve. Some recent examples have been a dear friend whose marriage is painfully disintegrating, a fellow believer choosing to walk away from the Lord, and a young mother of three suddenly diagnosed with stage 4 brain cancer. Where my help is woefully weak, each of those circumstances requires the Lord's strong hand to help. At times, I find myself tempted to worry about what will become of these souls. There are practical things that I can do, such as cooking a meal, advising marriage counseling, and inviting a doubting believer to discuss the scriptures together. But in the end, I cannot heal cancer, marriages, or wayward hearts. However, I can fast and pray. Being mindful of my weakness and God's strength is a refuge from my worries. There is something wonderful about remembering through my fasting and praying, that this is all I was given to do—the rest is up to the Lord's goodwill and power.

JUSTICE AND MERCY

> 6"Is not this the fast that I choose:
>   to loose the bonds of wickedness,
>   to undo the straps of the yoke,
> to let the oppressed go free,
>   and to break every yoke?

⁷*Is it not to share your bread with the hungry*
and bring the homeless poor into your house;
when you see the naked, to cover him,
and not to hide yourself from your own flesh?

As important as fasting is, these verses in Isaiah teach that fasting involves something more than just giving up food. According to verses 6 & 7, real fasting is a practical outpouring of a life dedicated to uphold justice and mercy. Going without food is a physical representation of what it means to give our lives for the sake of others. We can withhold our wants to provide for someone else's needs. This is surely a relief for anyone who is physically unable to fast but is still able to engage in acts of mercy, and a desperately needed reminder for us who can fast, to do both. Unhinged from a lifestyle of mercy and justice, fasting can quickly devolve into a religiously approved diet plan. This type of fasting, which is separated from worship of God and a life of service, makes quick work of developing arrogant, grumpy religious hypocrites as we see represented in verses 3 & 4.

A life focused on helping the poor and oppressed find mercy and justice is a life that focuses outside of oneself. Looking outside of our own lives and toward others can be a powerful way to release us from anxieties developed through inward self-obsession. For example, helping someone else financially can help ease our own fiscal anxieties. Often we find that we can happily live with less. Giving generously also helps reinforce to my heart that if God is able to use me to provide for someone else's needs, then he can lead someone else to provide for me in my need.

One difficulty in extending mercy and working towards justice, is that how much is needed can often feel overwhelming. I like to start with those directly in front of me, and trust the Lord to increase my awareness and ability as He sees fit. As a housewife, I personally employ three different people: a housecleaner, a babysitter, and an Arabic tutor for my children. These three different women have been in my home for years. I make every effort to pay them on time. I teach and enforce my children to speak with them respectfully. I enquire about their families and ask them about their lives, and when there is something pressing on their hearts, I have laid a hand on their shoulder and prayed for them. I am far from perfect, but looking at verse 7, I see the Lord's expectation of justice and mercy starts on a very personal, one-to-one level. Treating the few employees I have with just payment and merciful prayer is the bare minimum I can do as a follower of Jesus.

I will never cure cancer or end sex trafficking. But in my conduct to those nearest to me, I can strive to be as faithful as I can to imitate the justice and mercy that the Lord has shown me. We all have different spheres of influence. Some spheres, like mine, are small and intimate, while others may be quite extensive. I don't think the Lord is asking us to fulfill perfect justice and mercy to the entire world, but to be faithful to represent his justice and mercy in our own communities of influence.

Doing justice for others is a way of thinking of ourselves less, easing the mental strain of thinking and worrying about our own needs and future. It can be a powerful tool to break the self-deception that we are our own gods. When we give up our rights in order to raise up someone else, we pattern our lives after Jesus, who did not come to be served but to serve. And just like in fasting, we find that we can survive and even thrive while going without. In fasting we give up food to represent that we can freely give up all things to a Heavenly Father and lose nothing, just like we can give our time, gifts, mercy, meals, and hospitality to the poor and oppressed and find that we have gained the glory of the Lord.

Can you find even a hint of worry in verses 8-12? What are the cares of the man who the Lord guides continually, and who upholds your righteousness before you? Fasting humbles us before the Lord by remembering that we need him above all else. A lifestyle of mercy and justice helps us imitate the humility that Christ exemplified when he lived among us. Both practices work to help us remain in a restful state of humility before God.

A DELIGHTFUL SABBATH

> [13]"If you turn back your foot from the Sabbath,
> from doing your pleasure on my holy day,
> and call the Sabbath a delight
> and the holy day of the LORD honorable;
> if you honor it, not going your own ways,
> or seeking your own pleasure, or talking idly;
> [14]then you shall take delight in the LORD,
> and I will make you ride on the heights of the earth;
> I will feed you with the heritage of Jacob your father,
> for the mouth of the LORD has spoken."

Verses 13 & 14 show another example of how the religious people of Isaiah's day thought they were doing what was expected of them, only to find God's reprimand. As a person who has attended church my entire life, I find myself looking at this text with a wary and unsure heart. Doesn't going to church mean anything to God? Don't I get any participation points?!

I think that's what Isaiah is trying to communicate when he says we profane the Sabbath by doing our own pleasure. If we feel better by going to church because we've checked off something from our "things we're supposed to do list" and treat our attendance as though we've done the Lord a favor, then we have missed the delight of the Sabbath. This kind of sabbath-keeping seeks to give honor to ourselves, not to the Lord.

How then do we honor the Sabbath? I struggled with this when my three children were little. There were times when we attended church faithfully with a 3-year-old, a 2-year-old, and a newborn in tow. More than once I wondered if it would be more restful to stay at home and take a nap than to pack my family into church where I knew I would spend a significant amount of time settling someone in the nursery, changing diapers in the bathroom, trying to breast-feed someone discreetly, walking a stroller back and forth trying to settle someone, and generally trying to keep everyone (myself included) from crying.

I never stayed home for a nap, and each Sabbath I never regretted going. I think it took me those years of exhausted church attendance to realize why I needed an active church-attending Sabbath so much more than a nap. I realized that attending church answers four primary questions for me.

- Am I loved?
  The church affirms in all sorts of ways that I am loved by a Heavenly Father, as well as a family of believers, even if I only saw those fellow believers going in and out of the nursery.

- Do I matter?
  The church started long before me and will continue on into eternity. Everything I do to build and serve the church will have eternal significance. Even changing diapers of other people's children. I don't know what significance my life will hold at the end, but I know everything I've invested in the church will reap eternal dividends.

❧ Do I belong?

Relationships in the church are never perfect, but it is the best institution I know of that answers this question. Do you have an eternal soul?—then yes, you belong in church. You can be a part of this family, and you have a role to play.

❧ Am I good enough?

Faithfully the church answers this question for me with a resounding, 'Of Course Not!' And I need to hear it! She then gently adds, 'But Christ is enough for you; take his Righteousness and rest your weary soul.'

Even though my babies are older, I still find that it is rare that I get a chance to sit quietly during a church service, listen to the whole message, and sing all the songs. Yet, the time has refreshed and rested my anxious soul by affirming these four questions. I find that these questions are so central to my being that I need them affirmed regularly on weekly intervals. This affirmation gives me the rest my soul needs even more than eight consecutive hours of sleep. It pours cool waters over my hot anxious heart. It is an active rest, in that I have to remember, recall, sing, meditate, confess, listen, and take notes on what the Lord has done and is coming back to finish. This active rest is the only kind of rest truly effective to counteract worry and anxiety.

RESTORATIVE REPENTANCE

> 59:1Behold, the LORD's hand is not shortened, that it
> cannot save,
>   or his ear dull, that it cannot hear;

2but your iniquities have made a separation
  between you and your God,
and your sins have hidden his face from you
  so that he does not hear.

True repentance may be the most practical and obvious way to humble ourselves and avoid worry. Do you see what 59:1-2 are saying? God is fully capable of handling any difficulty in your life, but he chooses to ignore you when you choose to ignore Him.

Is it any wonder that Jesus starts his teaching ministry in Matthew with "Repent for the kingdom of God is at hand" (Matthew 4:17)? Repentance is always our first step with the Lord. The Christian life is a life of continual repentance.

I can think of nothing more worrying to me than to think that God does not hear my prayers. Likewise, I can think of nothing more comforting in the midst of stress than to know God does hear my prayers.

We are never to accept sin as a "natural" course of life; rather we are to live a life of repentance that acknowledges our need for a savior. If Christ is my Lord, then I do not have the freedom to accommodate, excuse, defend, or rationalize my sins. For example, what hope would I have in coming to God with my anxieties over my children, if I was unrepentantly engaging in gossip and slander of someone else? How could I hopefully pray for healing when I rationalize sexual immorality? If I defend my anger and irritability with my children, Isaiah 59:1-2 stands in between me and my prayers for financial worries.

Unrepentant sin is a curse that spreads and infects all areas of our lives. Repentance is the miracle elixir that turns us back toward God, to see his face and for him to hear our prayers.

GOSPEL TRUTH

Our text in Isaiah has given us four powerful and practical ways to humble ourselves before the Lord through fasting, a lifestyle of justice and mercy, delighting in the Sabbath, and keeping a short list of our unrepentant sins. And yet . . . the Israelites had these disciplines too, and they utterly failed. What hope do we have at doing any better? We have One Hope—the Gospel.

Let's continue in Isaiah 59:14-21:

> [14]*Justice is turned back,*
>   *and righteousness stands far away;*
> *for truth has stumbled in the public squares,*
>   *and uprightness cannot enter.*
> [15]*Truth is lacking,*
>   *and he who departs from evil makes himself a prey.*
>
> *The LORD saw it, and it displeased him*
>   *that there was no justice.*
> [16]*He saw that there was no man,*
>   *and wondered that there was no one to intercede;*
> *then his own arm brought him salvation,*
>   *and his righteousness upheld him.*
> [17]*He put on righteousness as a breastplate,*
>   *and a helmet of salvation on his head;*
> *he put on garments of vengeance for clothing,*
>   *and wrapped himself in zeal as a cloak.*
> [18]*According to their deeds, so will he repay,*
>   *wrath to his adversaries, repayment to his enemies;*
>   *to the coastlands he will render repayment.*
> [19]*So they shall fear the name of the LORD from the west,*
>   *and his glory from the rising of the sun;*
> *for he will come like a rushing stream,*
>   *which the wind of the LORD drives.*

^{20}*"And a Redeemer will come to Zion,*
> *to those in Jacob who turn from transgression,"*
> *declares the LORD.*

^{21}*"And as for me, this is my covenant with them," says the LORD:*
"My Spirit that is upon you, and my words that I have put in your
mouth, shall not depart out of your mouth, or out of the mouth of
your offspring, or out of the mouth of your children's offspring,"
says the LORD, "from this time forth and forevermore."

The Gospel is that God's Own Arm brought salvation. Isaiah saw a foreshadow of a Redeemer, but we have known the glory of the one who was crushed for our iniquities and bruised for our sins. Christ brought us the baptism of repentance, so we can ask the Lord in confidence to help us repent of our sins . . . and keep on repenting! Christ was the fulfillment of perfect Justice, so we can practice our fasting with humility and service, hoping not in our own abilities, but rather in his great help. And Christ is Lord of the Sabbath, so we can come to His church and experience his Rest.

The Gospel is that God has perfectly accomplished his work in Christ. This gives us the freedom to walk/stumble/crawl in our attempts towards fasting, justice, sabbath-keeping, and even repentance with the complete confidence that God does not look to us to perform these tasks with perfection, because he looks at Christ's performance in our place. From Christ, the Father commanded perfect justice for all transgressions, perfect righteousness in regards to the law, the purchase of eternal rest for all who believe, and to forge a new covenant sealed with the Holy Spirit of God. The Father's command to us is to follow the path Christ blazed, hope in his saving work, and find help and strength in his Spirit. How wonderful for us that the only one who is expected to be a Savior was Christ.

Start by doing small acts of justice, and see the Lord multiply your efforts. Fast and pray for the person or situation that is pressing on your heart. Faithfully attend a church and seek the Lord's help to serve and grow. Repent for the kingdom of God is at hand.

BIBLE STUDY

Week One

READING & REFLECTION

Read 1 Peter 5:6-7

Intro Question: What are some common causes for anxiety in our day?

Read Isaiah 58:1–59:2

1. Looking at 58:1-2, what kind of people are these?

2. (v. 3) How have they attempted to humble themselves?

3. Does anyone have any experiences of fasting?

4. How might fasting help with anxieties?

5. (v. 6-7) What does this kind of lifestyle look like practically?

6. Who are the people in your life that you could extend justice and mercy to?

7. How might religious fasting, without a lifestyle of mercy and justice, draw us further away from God?

8. How can practicing justice and mercy toward others help ease our own anxieties and worries of the future?

9. (v. 13) What does it mean to turn your back on the Sabbath?

10. How does honoring the Sabbath help us to take delight in the Lord?

11. (59:1-2) How does the Lord feel about unrepentant sin?

12. How does sinful living increase anxiety?

This text gives us four powerful preventative tools for avoiding some anxieties completely, and easing others: Fasting that seeks the face of God, Working for another's Justice, Honoring the Sabbath by actively remembering the Lord, and Repentance of sins that could cause God to hide his face from us.

As wonderful as these things are, and as effective as they are against anxiety, they are completely impossible for us to do. We are as utterly hopeless at doing these things as the original hearers of Isaiah's message. It is pure religion and not Gospel.

But we will find our hope by reading on in Isaiah 59:14-21.

13. Who is responsible for working out Justice?

14. Who is the only one who can bring our salvation?

15. (v. 21) What help do we now have to humble ourselves and to walk in humility towards the Lord?

CHALLENGE

Which of these areas of humility (fasting, justice & mercy, sabbath-keeping, and repentance) would you like to try to grow in this week?

Chapter Two

MEDITATING ON WHO GOD IS

Humble yourselves, therefore, **under the mighty hand of God** so that at the proper time he may exalt you, casting all your anxieties on him, because he cares for you.

1 Peter 5:6-7

WHAT IF PETER had written: "Humble yourselves, therefore, under God"? The text would be essentially the same, but what would we be missing? Or rather, what are we gaining by the description of God's Mighty Hand? Peter uses descriptive language of

God because our God is describable. Certainly there are aspects of him that are unknowable to us, however, the miracle is that the Creator of the Universe has revealed himself to creation and made himself known to man! Deuteronomy 29:29 reminds us, "The secret things belong to the LORD our God, but the things that are revealed belong to us and to our children forever, that we may do all the words of this law." God is not a 'life-force', or kharma, or 'the universe'; he is a knowable person with specific characteristics wanting to reveal himself to us for our good.

Peter's use of descriptive language toward God shows us that he is thinking about who God is and what he has done. This particular phrase, "the Mighty Hand of God," reminds biblical readers of the Exodus, bringing to mind his great work that he did in rescuing the Jews out of Egypt. The phrase "the mighty hand of God" was used several times in the Pentateuch in order to help the Israelites rightly remember and meditate on the importance of that event. In Deuteronomy 4:34, Moses implores his people to continue to worship God alone by expounding on the exodus, ". . . has any god ever attempted to go and take a nation for himself from the midst of another nation, by trials, by signs, by wonders, and by war, by a mighty hand and an outstretched arm, and by great deeds of terror, all of which the LORD your God did for you in Egypt before your eyes?"

The Israelites needed to remember that it was God who brought them out of Egypt, not themselves. It was God's Hand that crafted specific plagues to undermine Egyptian idol worship, and God's finger tips that played on the heartstrings of the Pharaoh. It was God's Mighty Hand that pushed aside the waters of the Red Sea and held it back for the people to walk upon dry ground, and it was his same mighty hand that brought the waters back, crushing the pursuing Egyptians.

Similarly, Peter's description of God's Mighty Hand, is meant to help us remember and think about the Lord's work in our own lives. His might is sufficient to save us from all slavery—just as it was for the Israelites in Egypt. And just as it was in Moses' time, God's hand is working for our good, providing our protection, lovingly caressing us, and administering needed discipline. Peter's brief description of God gives us insight into his mindset—which is a mindset that meditates on God.

CHRISTIAN MEDITATION

What does it mean to meditate on the Lord? Let's just clarify that Christian mediation is not the same as Eastern meditation. Eastern meditation seeks to bring peace of mind by emptying your mind of all thought. I suppose that may help to ease an anxious mind for that moment—but it is not enough to bring real peace of mind that can endure through life's harshest storms. Eventually, our minds will simply refill that empty space with the worries of the world.

Christian meditation is not the emptying of our minds of all our negative thoughts, rather it is thinking deeply about who God is and what he has done. It is chasing down every rabbit hole of our minds all the implications of what God has done and what it means for us. It means to consider all his ways, even those that are difficult understand. It is to think deeply about his character and who he is until we are blinded by his beauty. In a way, this study is a meditation on 1 Peter 5:6-7, in our attempts at dissecting all of its meaning, and by chasing down parallels in scripture to think and understand deeply what this verse means to us.

Let's look at another example of perhaps the best illustration of Christian meditation I know of in scripture, Psalm 103.

¹*Bless the LORD, O my soul,*
   and all that is within me,
   bless his holy name!
²*Bless the LORD, O my soul,*
   and forget not all his benefits,
³*who forgives all your iniquity,*
   who heals all your diseases,
⁴*who redeems your life from the pit,*
   who crowns you with steadfast love and mercy,
⁵*who satisfies you with good*
   so that your youth is renewed like the eagle's.
⁶*The LORD works righteousness*
   and justice for all who are oppressed.
⁷*He made known his ways to Moses,*
   his acts to the people of Israel.
⁸*The LORD is merciful and gracious,*
   slow to anger and abounding in steadfast love.
⁹*He will not always chide,*
   nor will he keep his anger forever.
¹⁰*He does not deal with us according to our sins,*
   nor repay us according to our iniquities.
¹¹*For as high as the heavens are above the earth,*
   so great is his steadfast love toward those who fear him;
¹²*as far as the east is from the west,*
   so far does he remove our transgressions from us.
¹³*As a father shows compassion to his children,*
   so the LORD shows compassion to those who fear him.
¹⁴*For he knows our frame;*
   he remembers that we are dust.

¹⁵*As for man, his days are like grass;*
   he flourishes like a flower of the field;
¹⁶*for the wind passes over it, and it is gone,*
   and its place knows it no more.

17But the steadfast love of the LORD is from everlasting to
everlasting on those who fear him,
and his righteousness to children's children,
18to those who keep his covenant
and remember to do his commandments.
19The LORD has established his throne in the heavens,
and his kingdom rules over all.

20Bless the LORD, O you his angels,
you mighty ones who do his word,
obeying the voice of his word!
21Bless the LORD, all his hosts,
his ministers, who do his will!
22Bless the LORD, all his works,
in all places of his dominion.
Bless the LORD, O my soul!

At first read, this psalm's exquisite beauty somewhat masks its meditative nature. It reads like a worship song, or a prayer—and unquestionably it should be used for both! However, the first verse tells us exactly who this psalm is addressed to—and it is not God. The psalmist is addressing his own soul. He is assuring himself of the nature of God and what God has done, then thinking out all of the implications of what that means for himself, his community, and the world. This is a meditation that digs deep into truth until it hits a wellspring of living waters to quench a thirsty soul.

MEDITATING ON GOD'S WORK IN MY LIFE

1Bless the LORD, O my soul,
and all that is within me,
bless his holy name!
2Bless the LORD, O my soul,

and forget not all his benefits,
    ³who forgives all your iniquity,
        who heals all your diseases,
    ⁴who redeems your life from the pit,
        who crowns you with steadfast love and mercy,
    ⁵who satisfies you with good
        so that your youth is renewed like the eagle's.

Who are the primary objects of his meditation in verses 1-5? Himself and the Lord. He starts where we all start—where is the Lord in my life? What has He done for me? Unless the Lord has parted the Red Sea before our eyes in the last 10 minutes, we are perilously prone to forget all His benefits. Spending time to remember what the Lord has done for us is essential to our spiritual well-being. I imagine the psalmist stating these out loud to himself—"the Lord has forgiven your iniquity, He has healed your diseases, He has redeemed your life"—and what starts as a list flourishes into descriptive metaphorical language: "He crowns you with steadfast love and mercy . . . your youth is renewed like the eagle's." What may have started as somewhat simple statements of what God has done, quickly turns poetic.

MEDITATING ON GOD IN THE COMMUNITY

As the psalmist continues his meditation, we see his vision expands. In verses 6-14 the psalmist's meditations extend to a community—specifically his own people. He recalls what the Lord has done for his own nation, remembering how God revealed himself to Moses through the Law and how He particularly chose the people of Israel. Now look at how verses 10-11 have expanded the summary in verse 3.

    ³who forgives all your iniquity

¹⁰*He does not deal with us according to our sins,*
   nor repay us according to our iniquities.
¹¹*For as high as the heavens are above the earth,*
   so great is his steadfast love toward those who fear him;
¹²*as far as the east is from the west,*
   so far does he remove our transgressions from us.

When his meditations continued and expanded so did his understanding of God. What started as a mere statement that God had forgiven his iniquities grew into one of the most beautiful descriptions in all of scriptures—that he has removed our transgressions as far as the east is from the west. Technically, verse 12 is not fundamentally different from verse 3, yet that same truth is expanded, explored and elaborated by continued meditation.

We will find a similar pattern in verses 5, and 13-14:

⁵*who satisfies you with good*
   so that your youth is renewed like the eagle's.

¹³*As a father shows compassion to his children,*
   so the LORD shows compassion to those who fear him.
¹⁴*For he knows our frame;*
   he remembers that we are dust.

In verse 5, it is stated that God will be good to us and renew our strength. But when the psalmist considered this truth in light of his meditations on God's nature within his community, he now understands that God is good to us, because He is our Father. He renews us, because He intimately knows our frailties, flaws, and muddy foundations. By expanding his meditations to what God has done not only for him, but for him and his community, the psalmist achieves broader understanding of God and sees more clearly God's relationship in that community, specifically as Father and Creator.

MEDITATING ON WHO GOD IS TO HUMANITY

We see the psalmists' thoughts shift again in verses 15-19, as his mind begins to consider not only what the Lord has done in his community, but also what he has done for all mankind: "As for man, his days are like grass." He is seeing the Lord not only as the God of Israel, but the Lord of ALL who fear him and call on him, and it brings him an even greater view of the Lord. Let's compare how his description of God's love has expanded through the progression of his meditations:

> *4who redeems your life from the pit,*
> *who crowns you with steadfast love and mercy,*

> *11For as high as the heavens are above the earth,*
> *so great is his steadfast love toward those who fear him;*

> *17But the steadfast love of the LORD is from everlasting to*
> *everlasting on those who fear him,*
> *and his righteousness to children's children,*

In verse 4, the psalmist understands that God gifts us his love and mercy, just like a crown of honor. In verse 11, we understand the immeasurable weight of that gift. Unlike human love, God's love has no limits nor restrictions, barring one—that we fear him alone. Which is another way of saying that we worship him alone. But then in verse 17, we are presented not only with the weight of his love, we are instructed that this love will extend to us from eternity to eternity. His desire is to love us unconditionally from now until forever, and that in this life, it will even overflow to our grandchildren. The psalmist has taken the truth, that God is Love, and turned it over and over again, until he has seen it from multiple angles and perspectives. He has thought on it until his thoughts reached to the heights of heavens and stretched to the everlastings.

MEDITATING ON THE LORD OF HEAVENS AND EARTH

> [20]Bless the LORD, O you his angels,
>   you mighty ones who do his word,
>   obeying the voice of his word!
> [21]Bless the LORD, all his hosts,
>   his ministers, who do his will!
> [22]Bless the LORD, all his works,
>   in all places of his dominion.
> Bless the LORD, O my soul!

Finally, the psalmist reaches the climax of his meditations. Peering into the very heights of heaven, he presumes to address even the angels (v. 20)! I am not sure that the psalmist even understands the depth of what he is saying, but his thoughts have carried him to extol that the Lord is in complete control of all angels, hosts and dominions. After establishing the boundless and eternal nature of God's love, he is now remembering that this same loving God is the power to which all other powers will submit. There is not an army that can stand against him; there is not a dominion that he does not control; there is not a power that can thwart his will.

How can any anxiety refuse to melt away under such marvelous knowledge? If we set our minds on these truths, what other cares and worries could we possibly have? Meditation does not distract us from the cares and worries of this life—it melts them under that white-hot knowledge of who God is and what he has done. If we are not swooning over the love that God has for us, then we have not taken time to think about how high the heavens are above the earth. If we do not feel perfectly safe and secure, then we have not put enough thought into the Lord who rules over all dominions, hosts, and powers in this world and in the heavens.

WE CAN CHOOSE WHAT WE MEDITATE ON

Whether we like it or not, we will all meditate on something. Our minds generally enjoy some kind of focused effort. In general, our inclination to meditate is a good thing, however, it can quickly turn to anxiety if the focus of our meditations are our fears.

I remember struggling with the constant anxiety that my husband would unexpectedly die while we were living outside the United States. I would mentally rehearse my worried questions over and over again. Where would we move? How would I raise my children alone? Could I sort out our finances in two different countries? It was a lingering anxiety that would often become more pronounced when my husband was away.

A few years ago, my husband was away for a week and fear gripped my mind. My thoughts were a whirling dervish of anxiety that I could not stop on my own. To make matters worse, our one and only vehicle had been in and out (but primarily in) a mechanic's garage for 5 months with numerous problems. Towards the end of this tortuous week, I found myself at church. I can't remember how, as I know that I didn't drive my own vehicle there, because the mechanic dropped our van off in the middle of the service.

After a relieving time in worship, I gathered my children into the car and hoped to return to some peaceful normalcy and drive home. But the car didn't start. And I cried miserably. I sat in the driver's seat feeling empty of all resources, with a rising fear of how I would get me and my children home. I then looked up and saw two men I knew. One was an elder and the other was the husband of a good friend of mine who had similar-aged children as mine. I looked at their pitying faces and realized in that moment, that they would not leave until I was settled and safe—at whatever cost of time and money. I knew that, because I knew that if my husband were standing in their shoes, that's what he would do, and has done in the past. I knew it was not because they were similar in personality to my husband, but that they had the same Holy Spirit that he did, which also stirred in them to help me. I saw my husband and the Lord in those men standing and waiting to help me, and my spirit calmed.

Shortly after, I realized that the mechanic had simply pulled on the parking brake (which I never use) and that my vehicle could actually drive. More importantly, I also realized that I was safe as the Lord's own—even if he should take my husband's life unexpectedly. I was not assured that my fear of my husband's death would never happen, however, I was assured that my fear of being abandoned never would. After that moment, each time I was tempted to meditate on that old fear, I would try to remember the godly men who patiently waited for me, while I figured out how to drive my car. I would then meditate on all the different families in the church I knew I could call to help me in an emergency situation. Finally, I would think back to all of the ways that God had provided for me unexpectedly and undeservedly. I kept thinking until I came to a place in my mind where I could finally agree with the saints that, "When peace like a river, attendeth my way, / When sorrows like sea billows roll; / Whatever my lot, Thou hast taught me to say, / It is well, it is well with my soul."

My mind did not suddenly stop worrying about the future, nor did my fearful thoughts magically stop spinning. However, by meditating on who the Lord is, and what He has done for me, I found a tool to help set my thoughts spinning in a completely different, anxiety-free direction. Meditating on how the Lord has worked in my community gave me some tangible hope to cling to. Considering how he knows the span of my days and even the hairs of my head gave me encouragement that he is in the midst of my struggles. Remembering that He is the Alpha and Omega to whom every power and principality is subject, that He upholds the universe by the word of His power, that He is coming again to judge the quick and the dead, makes it hard to worry about anything else.

Week Two

BIBLE STUDY

READING & REFLECTION

Read 1 Peter 5:6-7

Intro Question: What would be the difference in saying "Humble yourselves under God" vs. "Humble yourselves under the Mighty Hand of God"?

Read Psalm 103

1. Looking at v. 1-6, who is the psalmist talking to?

2. Who are the primary people of this section?

3. (v. 6-14) How have his meditations now changed?

4. How does the meditation of v. 10 & 11 help the meditation of v. 3?

5. How is v. 5 similar to v. 13 & 14? How do they expand each other?

6. How have the topics of the psalmists meditation expanded in v. 15?

7. How has his understanding of God's love expanded from v. 4 compared to v. 11 and then compared to v. 17?

8. In v. 20-22, where have the psalmist's thoughts taken him?

9. How does v. 22 expand v. 1?

10. How do v. 20-22 help ease our worries and anxieties of the future?

11. What do our minds naturally meditate on? Why is it sometimes easier to meditate on our fears than on God's promises?

12. How can we spend more time meditating on God? What are some practical ways?

CHALLENGE

What are some examples of God's faithfulness to you personally, and to your community, that you could meditate on to help ease current worries or anxieties?

Chapter Three

REASONABLE EXPECTATIONS

Humble yourselves, therefore, under the mighty hand of God **so that at the proper time he may exalt you,** *casting all your anxieties on him, because he cares for you.*

1 Peter 5:6-7

OUR EXPECTATIONS CAN have a significant impact on our anxieties. If we make assumptions on how things are supposed to be, only to find that our reality does not match our expectation, we can become anxious by thinking we are doing something wrong, or we are somehow missing out on something good.

I can remember one example where my expectations caused me unnecessary anxiety. While I was in college, I felt God calling me to live in the Middle East after I graduated. I had been interested in this for as long as I could remember, and it looked as if gaining a teaching certificate was a viable way to achieve my goals of living abroad.

I also had expectations that I would be married. Bound up within that expectation to be married were additional expectations that marriage would be the key to my joy, it would be the only way I would really be happy, and that it would exalt me. Whether or not I voiced these unrealistic expectations out loud and admitted them is another matter, but they were always lurking in the back corners of my mind. With those kinds of expectations, it is not hard to imagine that unnecessary anxieties were also on the way.

During my last year of university, I had committed myself to teaching for two years at a mission school in the Middle East. I was beyond excited! Shortly after I had made that commitment, I started dating a godly young man from my church. While dating this young man, it became clear that God was leading both of us in different directions; God was calling him to good works in the States, and God was leading me out to the Middle East. While there would appear to be an easy solution to this dilemma—amicably break up and follow the Lord's leading in our lives—I chose instead to live in a state of anxiety where I believed that I had to either choose to give up a dream of being married or a dream of following the Lord overseas. Because I was stubbornly holding on to my expectation of real happiness through marriage, and a lack of confidence in the Lord's ability to provide a husband while in the Middle East, I could not find the rest my heart craved.

Thankfully, my brother and the Lord intervened. In a frank and honest conversation my brother asked me if I really thought I would be happy staying in the relationship and settling in the states. While I respected the godly character of the man I was dating, I knew the answer was no. I knew I would be happier living out the adventure that God was calling me to. The Lord was also showing me that I could not put contingencies on how I followed and obeyed him. My heart was essentially telling the Lord, "I will follow your lead if you give me a husband." The Lord was graciously showing me that my obedience needed to be without exceptions and that he could be trusted to be the sole source of all my happiness and joy.

I found that my anxieties over moving overseas and over whether or not I would get married ceased when I learned to expect the Lord to be my joy. When The Holy One became my true husband, I did not feel anxious about missing out on marriage. When I expected my life to be used for the Lord's purposes instead of my own, I was released from the anxiety of an uncertain future. (My husband feels compelled to note here that I did, indeed, meet a dashing young man, who I met and married in less than a year.)

HOW HAS GOD EXALTED US?

1 Peter says that God will exalt us at the proper time, so it may be helpful to understand what exactly that means. Thankfully, the scriptures are not bashful or vague in describing how the Lord has honored us. Let's first look at a description of our exaltation from Ephesians 1:3-23. As you read it, either highlight with a pen or note in your mind each time Paul describes a way that we are honored, exalted, raised up, or elevated.

³Blessed be the God and Father of our Lord Jesus Christ, who has blessed us in Christ with every spiritual blessing in the heavenly places, ⁴even as he chose us in him before the foundation of the world, that we should be holy and blameless before him. In love ⁵he predestined us for adoption to himself as sons through Jesus Christ, according to the purpose of his will, ⁶to the praise of his glorious grace, with which he has blessed us in the Beloved. ⁷In him we have redemption through his blood, the forgiveness of our trespasses, according to the riches of his grace, ⁸which he lavished upon us, in all wisdom and insight ⁹making known to us the mystery of his will, according to his purpose, which he set forth in Christ ¹⁰as a plan for the fullness of time, to unite all things in him, things in heaven and things on earth.

¹¹In him we have obtained an inheritance, having been predestined according to the purpose of him who works all things according to the counsel of his will, ¹²so that we who were the first to hope in Christ might be to the praise of his glory. ¹³In him you also, when you heard the word of truth, the gospel of your salvation, and believed in him, were sealed with the promised Holy Spirit, ¹⁴who is the guarantee of our inheritance until we acquire possession of it, to the praise of his glory.

¹⁵For this reason, because I have heard of your faith in the Lord Jesus and your love toward all the saints, ¹⁶I do not cease to give thanks for you, remembering you in my prayers, ¹⁷that the God of our Lord Jesus Christ, the Father of glory, may give you the Spirit of wisdom and of revelation in the knowledge of him, ¹⁸having the eyes of your hearts enlightened, that you may know what is the hope to which he has called you, what are the riches of his glorious inheritance in the saints, ¹⁹and what is the immeasurable greatness of his power toward us who believe, according to the working of his great might ²⁰that he worked in Christ when he raised him from the dead and seated him at his right hand in the heavenly places, ²¹far above all rule and authority and power and dominion, and above every name that is named, not only in this

age but also in the one to come. ²²And he put all things under his feet and gave him as head over all things to the church, ²³which is his body, the fullness of him who fills all in all.

How many reasons did you find? I am sure whatever that number is, you could read the text again and still find another. Reading this text is like holding an enormous diamond in your hand. You can gaze at its beauty and think you've counted all its rainbows, but the moment you turn it you find new beautiful refractions of dancing light to amaze you. Just to point out a few gems: This text tells us that we have been honored as sons, adopted into the family of God (v. 5). We have been elevated to receive spiritual blessings in heavenly places (v. 3). We have been exalted in receiving an inheritance with Christ (v. 11), and we have been raised up beyond our abilities and understanding as we receive a spirit of wisdom and revelation in the knowledge of Christ (v. 16).

As this topic of how God has exalted us is so wonderful, let's look again at a parallel passage in Colossians 3:1-4.

¹If then you have been raised with Christ, seek the things that are above, where Christ is, seated at the right hand of God. ²Set your minds on things that are above, not on things that are on earth. ³For you have died, and your life is hidden with Christ in God. ⁴When Christ who is your life appears, then you also will appear with him in glory.

This passage is slightly less descriptive of how we will be exalted in Christ, however, it does give us some new insight as to when we will be exalted in Christ. We understand from this text that we are currently hidden in Christ (v. 3 & 4). Our souls are safe and secure, but we are not on display. Someone who is not hiding with us would not necessarily see the brilliance or glory of our new creation in Christ. However, there will be a day when we will be seen in all the glory that God has given to us—when Christ appears. When Christ's glory is on full display, our glory will be as well. If Christ has an appointed time to be exalted before all the nations, then we do as well. So that 'proper time when we will be exalted' that Peter is referring to, is the same time that Paul describes in v. 4: when Christ appears in glory, we will appear with him in glory as well.

WHAT ABOUT NOW?

If Christ's glorious return is the proper time for our exaltation, what do we make of today? Peter continues to give us helpful perspectives in order to manage our expectations and ease our anxieties. Let's read from 1 Peter 4:1-5.

> [1]Since therefore Christ suffered in the flesh, arm yourselves with the same way of thinking, for whoever has suffered in the flesh has ceased from sin, [2]so as to live for the rest of the time in the flesh no longer for human passions but for the will of God. [3]For the time that is past suffices for doing what the Gentiles want to do, living in sensuality, passions, drunkenness, orgies, drinking parties, and lawless idolatry. [4]With respect to this they are surprised when you do not join them in the same flood of debauchery, and they malign you; [5]but they will give account to him who is ready to judge the living and the dead.

Just as Christ will receive all glory and honor, he also endured an appointed time of suffering while on earth. Though some of his days were significantly worse than others, all of his days were led in patient endurance with this life. Peter reminds us to arm ourselves with the same mindset of Christ. He came to serve, not to be served. Service is messy, hard, draining, and often thankless. We must constantly remind ourselves that the time for serving our selfish interests and our human passions is gone. We should expect to suffer when we refuse to give in to the desires of our flesh, because it is the process of putting to death our fleshly nature. It is killing the part of us that is hostile to God. That is why Peter gives us encouragement in our sufferings that 'the one who suffers is done with sin'. It is not a meaningless pain to put to death our sinful nature; it is a suffering that will lead us to holiness. In one sense, feeling the sufferings of this life are an encouragement that we are meant for a different life. 1 Peter 4:12-19 continues to encourage us:

> [12]Beloved, do not be surprised at the fiery trial when it comes upon you to test you, as though something strange were happening to you. [13]But rejoice insofar as you share Christ's sufferings, that you may also rejoice and be glad when his glory is revealed. [14]If you are insulted for the name of Christ, you are blessed, because the Spirit of glory and of God rests upon you. [15]But let none of you suffer as a murderer or a thief or an evildoer or as a meddler. [16]Yet if anyone suffers as a Christian, let him not be ashamed, but let him glorify God in that name. [17]For it is time for judgment to begin at the household of God; and if it begins with us, what will be the outcome for those who do not obey the gospel of God? [18]And
>
> > "If the righteous is scarcely saved,
> > what will become of the ungodly and the sinner?"
>
> [19]Therefore let those who suffer according to God's will entrust their souls to a faithful Creator while doing good.

What a kindness this is, that the Father has given us! He is mercifully helping us to understand the times he has set, so that we can manage our expectations. Every suffering is meant for our good. If we suffer for doing wrong—then His purpose is to lead us to repentance. If we suffer for doing good, His purpose is to represent his Son and for us to share in his glory. He knows we will have to endure sufferings for a season, but he has promised to use them for his purpose to kill the sin in us AND to help us relate more to Christ. These are surely reasons enough for Peter to encourage us to rejoice, and examples of what Paul referred to as "the immeasurable greatness of his power toward us who believe, according to the working of his great might" (Ephesians 1:19)!

BEING WISE

When we understand what the purpose for suffering is in this life, and what glory is reserved for us in Christ's kingdom, we gain a freedom and joy that inherently repels anxieties and fears. When we train our minds to expect suffering and understand that it will be used for our good, then we no longer fear it. We can only start to put suffering into perspective after we start to consider how greatly the Lord will exalt us and honor us in his coming kingdom. Our current trials and tribulations are insignificant in comparison to the excessively great exaltation by the Father through the Son. When we live lives free from the fear and worry of suffering, we become explosively useful for kingdom work (Ephesians 5:15-17).

> *15Look carefully then how you walk, not as unwise but as wise, 16making the best use of the time, because the days are evil. 17Therefore do not be foolish, but understand what the will of the Lord is.*

We make wiser decisions about our time and lives when we no longer fear the loss or hope the gain of anything this life has to offer. We finally become efficient laborers in Christ's kingdom and not the world's. We can take huge Gospel risks, knowing that we are hidden in Christ. We can work for the good of those who despise us because we know that we are blessed in Christ with every spiritual blessing in the heavenly places. We can endure rejection because we know that we have been chosen and adopted by the author and maintainer of the entire universe. We can plant our lives and share the gospel in places of complete spiritual darkness because we know that there is an immeasurable greatness of his power toward us who believe in the one who is far above all rule and authority and power and dominion.

Week Three

BIBLE STUDY

READING & REFLECTION

Read 1 Peter 5:6-7

Intro Question: How can false expectations affect anxiety?

Read Ephesians 1:3-23

1. What are some of the ways God has exalted us or honored us from this passage?

Read Colossians 3:1-4

2. How does this text agree with the Ephesians text?

3. What new insight does it give us about our exaltation?

Read 1 Peter 4:1-5

4. In v. 1-5, what should we be preparing ourselves for, and why?

5. What should we be surprising the world with?

6. How does suffering help us overcome sin?

Read 1 Peter 4:12-19

7. What does suffering have the potential to do for us?

8. How does a proper view of suffering help us with anxiety?

9. What is the proper time we should expect to be exalted, and what should we expect now?

Read Ephesians 5:15-18

10. What does it mean to make the best use of our time?

11. How does a correct view of our suffering and our glory help us understand what the will of the Lord is today?

CHALLENGE

In light of our future glory in Christ, what are wise ways we can spend our lives now?

"They mistake who suppose that the highest happiness lies in wishes accomplished—in prosperity, wealth, favor, and success. There has been a joy in dungeons and on racks passing the joy of harvest. A joy strange and solemn, mysterious even to its possessor. A white stone dropped from the signet-ring, peace, which a dying Saviour took from his own bosom, and bequeathed to those who endure the cross, despising the shame."

—Harriet Beecher Stowe

Chapter Four

PRAYING OUR EMOTIONS

*Humble yourselves, therefore, under the mighty hand of God so that at the proper time he may exalt you, **casting all your anxieties on him,** because he cares for you.*

1 Peter 5:6-7

SOMETIMES OUR WORRIES and anxieties come in tsunamis. There are times when we have been working to practice all the disciplines of Christian life and follow closely to the will and work of Christ—and yet we feel as though we may be crushed underneath a storm custom made to undo us. During one particularly difficult period, when my husband and I didn't understand why the windstorms were blowing against us so incessantly, one friend reminded us of the promise from Isaiah 54:17—the idea that 'no weapon formed against you shall prosper' implies that there is a weapon that has been formed specifically for you. Somehow, understanding that though our storm was awful, it was not random brought comfort. It may have been designed specifically to undo us, but I knew that there was more than one manipulator of storms in the universe.

I was not comforted by thinking that I would come through the storm without any damage, but rather that I would not go through the storm alone. Despite the winds and waves, there was one whose eye was always on me and his voice created and still commands the deep waters of this world.

Up to this point, we have added quite a few tools to our belt that will help to lessen our anxiety. Tools such as fasting, repentance, sabbath worship, meditation, remembering our sufferings in context, etc. This week assumes that we have practiced these disciplines . . . and yet we still struggle with serious worries. What do we do when life's burdens simply feel too heavy for us to carry? For example, the anxiety of knowing a close family member who will not submit to the Lord, the death of a loved one, or strife in a marriage. Peter tells us in a rather succinct fashion to simply cast our cares on the Lord, a simple enough statement, however difficult to imagine what this means in practice. Thankfully, there is a whole book of the Bible devoted to the study of what it means to cast one's cares on the Lord in the midst of some of life's most harrowing storms. In order to gain insight on how to deal with some of our most deeply disturbing anxieties, we will look at someone who had more cares, sufferings, and anxieties than the vast majority of people who have lived, and how he gave them to the Lord.

Of all the souls that have lived and died on the earth, few could come close to comparing their sufferings with Job's. His story is in a complex and winding book of scripture. It is filled with old poetry, mysterious metaphors, haunting prophecy, and desperate prayer. Job is a book that comes alive when you feel close to death.

THE SUFFERING JOB

It can be easy to assume that the worries of our modern times are unique. We can mistakenly equate the less technological lives of those before us to have proportionally less anxieties. Less technology, however, does not equate to less complicated lives, nor fewer problems. So in case we mistake ourselves that our modern anxieties have evolved past that of a Middle Eastern man of antiquity, let's take a brief look at the one about whom God commended, "Have you considered the man Job?" (Job 1:1-5).

> *¹There was a man in the land of Uz whose name was Job, and that man was blameless and upright, one who feared God and turned away from evil. ²There were born to him seven sons and three daughters. ³He possessed 7,000 sheep, 3,000 camels, 500 yoke of oxen, and 500 female donkeys, and very many servants, so that this man was the greatest of all the people of the east. ⁴His sons used to go and hold a feast in the house of each one on his day, and they would send and invite their three sisters to eat and drink with them. ⁵And when the days of the feast had run their course, Job would send and consecrate them, and he would rise early in the morning and offer burnt offerings according to the number of them all. For Job said, "It may be that my children have sinned, and cursed God in their hearts." Thus Job did continually.*

Notice, even in the very beginning of the story—before any overt spiritual attack—Job is dealing with daily anxiety. He lives in constant concern over his children's spiritual well-being and their standing before God. As a mother, I can completely relate to Job's concern, and I can learn from this man who takes that anxiety and offers it in sacrifice to the Lord early each morning. He has established a pattern to handle the every day anxieties of his life, which is centered around his worship of God.

Job then faces an example of what Isaiah meant by "weapons formed against you". Job's persecutions were pre-planned, thought through, and masterfully executed. Job does not have bad luck; he has an adversary. Satan meticulously crafts a Job-specific weapon intent on destroying his soul. Read Job 1:13-22.

> [13]Now there was a day when his sons and daughters were eating and drinking wine in their oldest brother's house, [14]and there came a messenger to Job and said, "The oxen were plowing and the donkeys feeding beside them, [15]and the Sabeans fell upon them and took them and struck down the servants with the edge of the sword, and I alone have escaped to tell you." [16]While he was yet speaking, there came another and said, "The fire of God fell from heaven and burned up the sheep and the servants and consumed them, and I alone have escaped to tell you." [17]While he was yet speaking, there came another and said, "The Chaldeans formed three groups and made a raid on the camels and took them and struck down the servants with the edge of the sword, and I alone have escaped to tell you." [18]While he was yet speaking, there came another and said, "Your sons and daughters were eating and drinking wine in their oldest brother's house, [19]and behold, a great wind came across the wilderness and struck the four corners of the house, and it fell upon the young people, and they are dead, and I alone have escaped to tell you."

20Then Job arose and tore his robe and shaved his head and fell on the ground and worshiped. 21And he said, "Naked I came from my mother's womb, and naked shall I return. The Lord gave, and the Lord has taken away; blessed be the name of the Lord."

22In all this Job did not sin or charge God with wrong.

The first attack of Satan's supernatural weapon resulted in Job's abject poverty and the death of his 7 children. Many of us stumble hard over the loss of a job or the loss of a single loved one; Job's loss is almost beyond our ability to imagine. Not only are his children all dead, he does not even have the consolation of knowing where their hearts stood before the Lord. Job was living in his own personal atomic bomb. However, the attack isn't finished; we read his second assault in Job 2:7-10.

7So Satan went out from the presence of the Lord and struck Job with loathsome sores from the sole of his foot to the crown of his head. 8And he took a piece of broken pottery with which to scrape himself while he sat in the ashes.

9Then his wife said to him, "Do you still hold fast your integrity? Curse God and die." 10But he said to her, "You speak as one of the foolish women would speak. Shall we receive good from God, and shall we not receive evil?" In all this Job did not sin with his lips.

Just as an atomic bomb leaves behind lingering lethal radioactivity, the assault on Job's soul left continual suffering of chronic health issues and a strained marriage. Even in our times, it is not difficult to see connections between poverty and sickness, or the loss of children and divorce. I can imagine, of the two, the loss of support from his spouse hurt worse. Physical pain is bearable with a loved one. But to find the one you have loved, served, laughed, and raised children with, turn to you with disdain in her voice—is a wound far more painful than any sword could inflict.

So to count up the troubles of Job's life thus far, we have: anxiety over his children's salvation, the sudden death of seven children, economic devastation, a mysterious chronic disease, and a strained marriage. Maybe you can identify with one or more of Job's troubles, as it appears that he has struggled with every serious heartbreak in the modern (and ancient) world. Surely we could learn something from this man on how to handle our anxieties.

THE RELATABLE JOB

One thing I appreciate about Job's narrative is that he speaks like I do when I am feeling depressed, which primarily sounds like angry and confused rants. God did not ask Job if it would be okay to use him as an object lesson on how to suffer, nor ask his permission to make Job a pillar for all humanity to look to in the midst of their suffering. Job couldn't flip to the last chapter of his life to see how all of his afflictions would end in an expression of God's glory. In Job 1:6-11, we see he simply suffered in ignorance.

6Now there was a day when the sons of God came to present themselves before the Lord, and Satan also came among them. 7The Lord said to Satan, "From where have you come?" Satan answered the Lord and said, "From going to and fro on the earth, and from walking up and down on it." 8And the Lord said to Satan, "Have you considered my servant Job, that there is none like him on the earth, a blameless and upright man, who fears God and turns away from evil?" 9Then Satan answered the Lord and said, "Does Job fear God for no reason? 10Have you not put a hedge around him and his house and all that he has, on every side? You have blessed the work of his hands, and his possessions have

*increased in the land. ¹¹But stretch out your hand and touch all
that he has, and he will curse you to your face."*

Although Job is ignorant of the causes of his sufferings, to his credit he knows that God is not. Job was not privy to the conversation between The Author of Good and the Instigator of Evil about the upcoming events in his life. However, Job fully understood that all of his experiences, be they sorrow or joy, have passed under the authority of God. We see this in his initial response in Job 1:21, "The Lord gives and the Lord takes away." He does not curse the devil, or lament that God was not strong enough to fight on his behalf—rather he starts processing his suffering firmly established in the sovereignty of God over all things seen and unseen. No weapon formed against Job could knock him off of this rock. It is the same rock which Jesus advised to build one's life on, as opposed to shifting sands, in Matthew 7:24. Jesus knew that storms would come, but the foundations on which we have built our lives would determine whether we would be swept away when the billows roll, or endure till the winds and waves have ceased. Job had lost everything except his hope in God's complete sovereignty. It is from this position that Job begins to wrestle with the Lord about his sufferings, and I believe it is also the place where we must wrestle with the Lord in ours.

THE PRAYING JOB

After the dust settled from the demolition of Job's life, he began to process his sufferings. Like all of us who have lamented through a crushing blow, his words ramble through expressions of depression, anger, confusion, and occasional hope. Sometimes he is talking to himself, other times to his friends, but all his speech contains a posture of prayer. Job is ultimately talking to God, knowing that He hears him, and it is from Him that he is searching for answers. Let's read one example below from Job 19:

1Then Job answered and said:

2"How long will you torment me
and break me in pieces with words?
3These ten times you have cast reproach upon me;
are you not ashamed to wrong me?
4And even if it be true that I have erred,
my error remains with myself.
5If indeed you magnify yourselves against me
and make my disgrace an argument against me,
6know then that God has put me in the wrong
and closed his net about me.
7Behold, I cry out, 'Violence!' but I am not answered;
I call for help, but there is no justice.
8He has walled up my way, so that I cannot pass,
and he has set darkness upon my paths.
9He has stripped from me my glory
and taken the crown from my head.
10He breaks me down on every side, and I am gone,
and my hope has he pulled up like a tree.
11He has kindled his wrath against me
and counts me as his adversary.
12His troops come on together;
they have cast up their siege ramp against me
and encamp around my tent.

13"He has put my brothers far from me,
and those who knew me are wholly estranged from me.
14My relatives have failed me,
my close friends have forgotten me.
15The guests in my house and my maidservants count me

as a stranger;

    I have become a foreigner in their eyes.

¹⁶I call to my servant, but he gives me no answer;

    I must plead with him with my mouth for mercy.

¹⁷My breath is strange to my wife,

    and I am a stench to the children of my own mother.

¹⁸Even young children despise me;

    when I rise they talk against me.

¹⁹All my intimate friends abhor me,

    and those whom I loved have turned against me.

²⁰My bones stick to my skin and to my flesh,

    and I have escaped by the skin of my teeth.

²¹Have mercy on me, have mercy on me, O you my friends,

    for the hand of God has touched me!

²²Why do you, like God, pursue me?

    Why are you not satisfied with my flesh?

²³"Oh that my words were written!

    Oh that they were inscribed in a book!

²⁴Oh that with an iron pen and lead

    they were engraved in the rock forever!

²⁵For I know that my Redeemer lives,

    and at the last he will stand upon the earth.

²⁶And after my skin has been thus destroyed,

    yet in my flesh I shall see God,

²⁷whom I shall see for myself

    and my eyes shall behold, and not another.

    My heart faints within me!

²⁸If you say, 'How we will pursue him!'

    and, 'The root of the matter is found in him,'

²⁹be afraid of the sword,

    for wrath brings the punishment of the sword,

    that you may know there is a judgment."

If you have never felt your hope pulled up like a tree, then these words may sound foreign or exaggerated. But for those who have, reading Job's lament before God can feel like relief. Job doesn't hide himself or how he feels, but gives full expression of his emotional state before God. Job does not ignore God when he is hurt, but rather comes closer and focuses his rants up at him! Even though Job feels like God "has counted him as an adversary" (v. 11), he still calls out to him and longs to see him (v. 26).

Job takes all his hurts, his anxieties, his sufferings and he lists them in an angry prayer before the Lord. He sits under the mighty hand of God and he cries out, stomps his feet, moans, and even whimpers. But he never turns away from the Lord. God is present in every expression of his wretchedness. Job sits on the rock of God's sovereignty, knowing that every misery of his life is seen by the God who has every power to intervene, and howls out that 'it's not fair!' Amazingly we find in the book of Job, that God approves of his behavior! Read Job 42:7-8.

> *7After the Lord had spoken these words to Job, the Lord said to Eliphaz the Temanite: "My anger burns against you and against your two friends, for you have not spoken of me what is right, as my servant Job has. 8Now therefore take seven bulls and seven rams and go to my servant Job and offer up a burnt offering for yourselves. And my servant Job shall pray for you, for I will accept his prayer not to deal with you according to your folly. For you have not spoken of me what is right, as my servant Job has."*

That is not to say that Job was correct in all that he prayed. Clearly in Job 19:8-11, God did not make Job his enemy, nor was it the Lord who had set darkness over his path. We know that was Satan's plan for Job, not God's. God does not condemn Job for his poor understanding of his sufferings, but rather I believe God has given us Job's bitter prayers as an example to show that we do not have to be afraid to draw near to God in our pain. In our deepest anxieties and our darkest sufferings, God is not phased by our angry tantrums, as long as we tantrum in his presence. Job did not take the advice of his wife and curse God. He neither rejected God in his suffering nor stopped talking with him. Rather, Job worked through his suffering in the presence and knowledge of God, and so must we. He cast the great burden of his cares upon the Lord in relentless, emotional prayer.

Just as he did with Job, God is able to bring us to a place of hope no matter how terrible our circumstances. We see in Job 19:25 the storm clouds of anger break up and a ray of sun shines through. Even though Job accuses God of treating him like an enemy, he still hopes in God for a living Redeemer. He sees clearly his need for someone stronger than himself, to intercede for him and bring him to God. God revealed a reason for hope to Job, a prophecy for an intercessor between heaven and earth. God offers us something even better: the fulfillment of that prophecy in Christ.

A BETTER JOB

Job understood acutely that sometimes bad things happen to good people. Sometimes godly people suffer when they do not deserve it. Job shows us how a good Christ would come to suffer evil.

Sometimes our sufferings are of our own making, and repentance is the biblical prescription to heal those self-inflicted wounds. But sometimes our sufferings are simply because we follow a God who suffered himself. We may not get explanations that will satisfy our minds, but we have been given a living example that can satisfy our hearts. There was one who suffered and it was not his fault. Job may have been wrong in some of his accusations about God's treatment of him, but let's read some of his words again, imagining we are sitting outside on a dark night in the Garden of Gethsemane as we reimagine Job 19 as the prayer of Christ:

Father, I know that you have put me in the wrong in the place of others, and you are closing your net about me. You have stripped me of my glory and taken the crown from my head. You will break me down on every side. Your wrath is kindled against me and instead of counting me a Son, you will count me your adversary.

Even my brothers are far from me! Those who knew me are wholly estranged from me! My own relatives have failed me, my close friends forgotten me. All my intimate friends abhor me, and those whom I love have turned against me. My bones stick to my skin and to my flesh.

Yet I know that I am the Redeemer who lives. In the end I will stand on the earth. After my skin has been destroyed, yet in my flesh I shall see God.

God was never an enemy of Job's. But Christ became an enemy of God, when he stood in our place to take the full wrath of God for all our offenses. Christ was stripped of his Glory, so that after our flesh is destroyed, we could see God. God kindled his wrath against the Son, so that he could embrace us as his children.

Now, as we pray in our own Garden of Gethsemane, in our places of deepest hurt and confusion, we know we are not alone. As we are casting our anxieties on Him, we know we have a high priest who is able to sympathize with our weaknesses. One who was tempted in every respect, yet without sin. So that we can confidently draw near to the throne of grace with all our tears, with all our irritable moods, our indignation, our unanswered questions, our deepest wounds, and find mercy and grace to help in time of need.

Week Four

BIBLE STUDY

READING & REFLECTION

Read 1 Peter 5:6-7

Intro Questions: What is a summary of the ways that we have dealt with anxiety so far? Which have been new to you? Which have been the most practical?

Read Job 1:1-5

1. What were the cares, worries, anxieties, and sufferings that Job may have experienced according to these passages?

Read Job 1:13-22 and Job 2:7-10

2. Which of Job's anxieties were the result of the Satanic attack and which of his anxieties and sufferings were the result of normal living?

Read Job 1:6-11

3. What did Job do to deserve his sufferings?

4. Which of Job's sufferings and anxieties do you find it easiest to relate to?

Read Job 19

    5.   What is Job's mood in these texts?

    6.   What are his emotions?

    7.   To whom is he talking?

    8.   What does Job get right and what does he get wrong?

Read Job 42:7-8

    9.   Why do you think Job is commended?

    10. How were Job and Christ similar?

    11. How does Job's story help us understand Christ's story better?

CHALLENGE

What emotions are we repressing that we should be processing with God? How can we begin to process our difficult emotions?

Chapter Five

EXAMINING OUR SALVATION

Humble yourselves, therefore, under the mighty hand of God so that at the proper time he may exalt you, casting all your anxieties on him, **because he cares for you.**

1 Peter 5:6-7

I SUSPECT THAT at the core of all of our fears and anxieties is an unsettled question of, 'Am I really loved?'. Sometimes we will settle for answers to sub-questions of this, such as 'Am I worthwhile?', 'Am I respected?', 'Am I valuable?'.

We can try to answer these questions through vehicles of family, work, ambition, charity, politics, etc. However, the irony is that the more that we look for the answer to the question of 'Am I loved?' in these other areas of our lives, the more these areas will cause us anxiety, fear, worry, and anger. There is only one person that we can safely look to for the answer our soul craves and He shouted the answer in the greatest event the universe has ever known.

One reason that our successes in work, marriage, family, politics, and philanthropy cannot answer our heart's deep-rooted questions of our value, worth, and love is because they cannot give an answer clear enough or loud enough. Looking for answers in these areas are at best interpretive, fickle, changing, and quiet. We can often end up with mixed answers like these:

> I spent this entire month teaching my child not to bite other children; does that make me a valuable person to society? Even though I have done absolutely nothing to end world poverty?!?

> I feel I am respected for my work in clean water initiatives, however, my heart aches when I think about how much time I have spent away from my family. Will those balance out?

Joyfully, there is one place that we can look, that can clearly answer the question of our heart. If we look towards Golgotha, we will find the Maker of heaven and earth, waving banners of his love, affection, acceptance, and care for us.

I love how the musical artist The Silver Pages summarized it in their song, "He Shouted Love"—

> *God didn't whisper 'I love you' from heaven,*
> *He shouted love from on the cross.*

We don't have to interpret it, we don't have to assume an unspoken love, we don't have to hope to understand it. We only have to look at the cross, where we can clearly and confidently see that God cares for us. When we are looking at the cross, the volume of how loud God is shouting his love for us completely drowns out the anxieties, fears, and worries of all the other areas of our life.

BEYOND SUNDAY SCHOOL UNDERSTANDING

Maybe some of you dear readers are like me, and you never knew a time when the phrase "Jesus died on the cross for my sins" was not a bedrock fact in your mind. I grew up with this truth from the time I was in diapers and the veracity of that statement was always as real to me as 'the sky is blue'. While I am more than thankful for that kind of upbringing, I realize that there can be a temptation to think, "Yes, yes, I understand the cross, but I need something more to help me with my current circumstances."

To counter this thinking, let's look briefly at a side comment Peter makes about the Gospel in 1 Peter 1:10-12:

> [10]Concerning this salvation, the prophets who prophesied about the grace that was to be yours searched and inquired carefully, [11]inquiring what person or time the Spirit of Christ in them was indicating when he predicted the sufferings of Christ and the subsequent glories. [12]It was revealed to them that they were serving not themselves but you, in the things that have now been announced to you through those who preached the good news to you by the Holy Spirit sent from heaven, things into which angels long to look.

Peter is attempting to communicate that our current salvation in Christ was the hope that all prophets strained to see. Yet he casually mentions that the angels in heaven look at our salvation with longing. The angels are mesmerized by the work of Christ. The Gospel captivates them and the beauty of it consumes them. If angels are far smarter than I am, and they do not tire to look upon the work and means of my salvation, then I would also do well to continually gaze at this great salvation.

GAZING DEEPLY INTO THE CROSS

We will continue to have a basic and shallow appreciation of the gospel, if we—unlike the angels—cease to gaze upon it and meditate upon its implications for us. If we never wrestle with our salvation, examine it and work it out, we will never understand its depths. Unarguably, the death and resurrection of Jesus changed the scope of human history like no other single event. Just thinking about the historical implications of the cross can take a lifetime. And while Christ's death on a cross was a historical event, for us who believe it is much more significantly a spiritual event.

The gospel is whispered, implied, hinted, forecasted, prophesied, and plainly written throughout all of scripture. I have picked three passages for us to examine, but they are by no means exhaustive of all we can learn on the death and resurrection. They are only a beginning towards an eternity of understanding.

We will begin with Psalm 22, the psalm which was on our Lord's heart and lips while hanging on the cross.

> *1My God, my God, why have you forsaken me?*
> *Why are you so far from saving me, from the words of*
> *my groaning?*
> *2O my God, I cry by day, but you do not answer,*
> *and by night, but I find no rest.*
> *3Yet you are holy,*
> *enthroned on the praises of Israel.*

⁴In you our fathers trusted;
   they trusted, and you delivered them.
⁵To you they cried and were rescued;
   in you they trusted and were not put to shame.

⁶But I am a worm and not a man,
   scorned by mankind and despised by the people.
⁷All who see me mock me;
   they make mouths at me; they wag their heads;
⁸"He trusts in the Lord; let him deliver him;
   let him rescue him, for he delights in him!"

⁹Yet you are he who took me from the womb;
   you made me trust you at my mother's breasts.
¹⁰On you was I cast from my birth,
   and from my mother's womb you have been my God.
¹¹Be not far from me,
   for trouble is near,
   and there is none to help.

¹²Many bulls encompass me;
   strong bulls of Bashan surround me;
¹³they open wide their mouths at me,
   like a ravening and roaring lion.
¹⁴I am poured out like water,
   and all my bones are out of joint;
my heart is like wax;
   it is melted within my breast;
¹⁵my strength is dried up like a potsherd,
   and my tongue sticks to my jaws;
   you lay me in the dust of death.

¹⁶For dogs encompass me;
   a company of evildoers encircles me;
they have pierced my hands and feet—

> [17]I can count all my bones—
>   they stare and gloat over me;
> [18]they divide my garments among them,
>   and for my clothing they cast lots.

This psalm gives insight to the emotional state of Christ on the cross, as well as specific prophecies of what would happen to him. We see in verses 14 and 15 that the Psalmist is prophesying extreme physical distress, exhaustion, and even thirst. Verses 16 and 17 become even more specific with the description of a man whose hands and feet have been pierced, and despite extreme physical abuse, no bones are broken. Finally, in verse 18 we see an oddly specific comment about the fate of the sufferer's clothes, which may have felt a bit odd to the original readers to include in the list of sufferings after such a detailed description of the sufferings of his body.

Personally, I am so thankful for the specific details about the physical occurrences on the crucifixion. It helps me take greater confidence in the harder-to-visualize spiritual realities that occurred on the cross. Christ didn't quote verse 18 from the cross, as he watched the soldiers throw dice for his clothes. He quoted verse 1—that he was being forsaken by God. His eternal Father was now distant to him. The one with whom he had enjoyed a continual and perfect relationship from eternity past was forsaking him. In procuring our salvation, Christ suffered rejection from the Father, so that we could be adopted by him. Our salvation was not primarily bought by Christ's physical sufferings, as great as they were, but his spiritual sufferings, which took the complete rejection of God in our place so that we would be able to enjoy his complete acceptance in Christ.

Let's continue our salvific examination reading Isaiah 53.

¹Who has believed what he has heard from us?
    And to whom has the arm of the Lord been revealed?
²For he grew up before him like a young plant,
    and like a root out of dry ground;
he had no form or majesty that we should look at him,
    and no beauty that we should desire him.
³He was despised and rejected by men,
    a man of sorrows and acquainted with grief;
and as one from whom men hide their faces
    he was despised, and we esteemed him not.

⁴Surely he has borne our griefs
    and carried our sorrows;
yet we esteemed him stricken,
    smitten by God, and afflicted.
⁵But he was pierced for our transgressions;
    he was crushed for our iniquities;
upon him was the chastisement that brought us peace,
    and with his wounds we are healed.
⁶All we like sheep have gone astray;
    we have turned—every one—to his own way;
and the Lord has laid on him
    the iniquity of us all.

⁷He was oppressed, and he was afflicted,
    yet he opened not his mouth;
like a lamb that is led to the slaughter,
    and like a sheep that before its shearers is silent,
    so he opened not his mouth.
⁸By oppression and judgment he was taken away;
    and as for his generation, who considered
that he was cut off out of the land of the living,
    stricken for the transgression of my people?
⁹And they made his grave with the wicked

and with a rich man in his death,
although he had done no violence,
    and there was no deceit in his mouth.

10 Yet it was the will of the Lord to crush him;
    he has put him to grief;
when his soul makes an offering for guilt,
    he shall see his offspring; he shall prolong his days;
the will of the Lord shall prosper in his hand.
11 Out of the anguish of his soul he shall see and be
satisfied; by his knowledge shall the righteous one,
my servant,
    make many to be accounted righteous,
    and he shall bear their iniquities.
12 Therefore I will divide him a portion with the many,
    and he shall divide the spoil with the strong,
because he poured out his soul to death
    and was numbered with the transgressors;
yet he bore the sin of many,
    and makes intercession for the transgressors.

In a similar way to Psalm 22, this passage gives very specific prophecies as well as spiritual explanations. For example, verses 4, 5, & 7 give a detailed prophecy describing the emotional, psychological and physical sufferings of the Messiah. We know he will be rejected and despised, he will be crushed and stricken, and amazingly, we see a confirmation from Psalm 22 that he will be pierced. We see as well that he will go to his death without resistance, as a lamb goes to the slaughter.

In verse 6 we gain insight as to the reason for all of this suffering. The Lord was laying on him the iniquity of us all. The Messiah was to be a substitutionary sacrifice for our sins. He was to die in our place. The fulfillment of the physical death and sufferings of Christ, confirm for us that in the spiritual realm, God the Father did indeed lay all our iniquities on Christ the Son. Verses 10 and 11 reveal to us that it was the will of the Father to crush his beloved and innocent Son with the wrath he had for our sins. The Son was satisfied to take this crushing blow in order to purchase our righteousness. This is the cost of our forgiveness. This is the price paid for our righteousness. And by purifying our souls with his blood, he made it possible for the Holy Spirit to dwell in and intercede for us. This is the love that the Triune God extends to us.

For us who live after the events of the death and resurrection of Jesus, these passages are plain to interpret. It is with extreme thankfulness that we can understand the full realities of Psalm 22 and Isaiah 53 because we live after the event described in Matthew 27:27-60:

Jesus Is Mocked

[27]Then the soldiers of the governor took Jesus into the governor's headquarters, and they gathered the whole battalion before him. [28]And they stripped him and put a scarlet robe on him, [29]and twisting together a crown of thorns, they put it on his head and put a reed in his right hand. And kneeling before him, they mocked him, saying, "Hail, King of the Jews!" [30]And they spit on him and took the reed and struck him on the head. [31]And when they had mocked him, they stripped him of the robe and put his own clothes on him and led him away to crucify him.

The Crucifixion

[32]As they went out, they found a man of Cyrene, Simon by name. They compelled this man to carry his cross. [33]And when they came to a place called Golgotha (which means Place of a Skull), [34]they offered him wine to drink, mixed with gall, but when he tasted it, he would not drink it. [35]And when they had crucified him, they

divided his garments among them by casting lots. ³⁶Then they sat down and kept watch over him there. ³⁷And over his head they put the charge against him, which read, "This is Jesus, the King of the Jews." ³⁸Then two robbers were crucified with him, one on the right and one on the left. ³⁹And those who passed by derided him, wagging their heads ⁴⁰and saying, "You who would destroy the temple and rebuild it in three days, save yourself! If you are the Son of God, come down from the cross." ⁴¹So also the chief priests, with the scribes and elders, mocked him, saying, ⁴²"He saved others; he cannot save himself. He is the King of Israel; let him come down now from the cross, and we will believe in him. ⁴³He trusts in God; let God deliver him now, if he desires him. For he said, 'I am the Son of God.'" ⁴⁴And the robbers who were crucified with him also reviled him in the same way.

The Death of Jesus

⁴⁵Now from the sixth hour there was darkness over all the land until the ninth hour. ⁴⁶And about the ninth hour Jesus cried out with a loud voice, saying, "Eli, Eli, lema sabachthani?" that is, "My God, my God, why have you forsaken me?" ⁴⁷And some of the bystanders, hearing it, said, "This man is calling Elijah." ⁴⁸And one of them at once ran and took a sponge, filled it with sour wine, and put it on a reed and gave it to him to drink. ⁴⁹But the others said, "Wait, let us see whether Elijah will come to save him." ⁵⁰And Jesus cried out again with a loud voice and yielded up his spirit.

⁵¹And behold, the curtain of the temple was torn in two, from top to bottom. And the earth shook, and the rocks were split. ⁵²The tombs also were opened. And many bodies of the saints who had fallen asleep were raised, ⁵³and coming out of the tombs after his resurrection they went into the holy city and appeared to many. ⁵⁴When the centurion and those who were with him, keeping watch over Jesus, saw the earthquake and

what took place, they were filled with awe and said, "Truly this was the Son of God!"

⁵⁵There were also many women there, looking on from a distance, who had followed Jesus from Galilee, ministering to him, ⁵⁶among whom were Mary Magdalene and Mary the mother of James and Joseph and the mother of the sons of Zebedee.

Jesus Is Buried

⁵⁷When it was evening, there came a rich man from Arimathea, named Joseph, who also was a disciple of Jesus. ⁵⁸He went to Pilate and asked for the body of Jesus. Then Pilate ordered it to be given to him. ⁵⁹And Joseph took the body and wrapped it in a clean linen shroud ⁶⁰and laid it in his own new tomb, which he had cut in the rock. And he rolled a great stone to the entrance of the tomb and went away.

Have you heard the shouts of love? Did you calculate your value by the price that was spent to buy you? Did you see how you were cared for? Could you possibly read these passages and think "Yes . . . Christ gave all that but he left out (—&—) and this is the cause of my anxiety"? No. There is nothing Christ kept from us. He was forsaken by his heavenly Father so that we could call God "Our Father who art in Heaven". He felt the silence of God, so that God could hear our prayers. He was pierced, chastised, bruised and crushed, so that God would not have to show to us the wrath our sins deserved. His blood was drained, so that we could be a cleansed temple of the Holy Spirit. Amazingly, Christ was satisfied with his payment—in order to call us his brothers! There is nothing that we need that was not bought at the crucifixion. And we know that the payment was accepted, and there are no outstanding debts, because after giving his life for the salvation of all mankind— God raised him from the dead as proof that 'It is finished.'

DEFINING OUR SALVATION

We have just gazed deeply at the cross, and it is akin to gazing at the sun. Its brilliance is blinding and beautiful. Sometimes we can appreciate the sun more by reflecting on all that we gain by it, such as the growth of fruits and vegetables, vitamin D, warmth, light, energy, the gravitational rotation of our planet earth, etc. We cannot overstate the significance that the sun has on our ability to physically live on earth.

In an even greater way, we cannot overstate the significance of the work that was done on the Cross. Christ's death has bought for us:

- Forgiveness of sins *and* the imputed righteousness of Christ's holy life
- New creation unfettered by slavery to sin
- Indwelling and gifts of the Holy Spirit
- Adoption as sons of God
- Eternal life in the presence of God

Considering the significance and cost of these free gifts of our salvation, their worth and value is almost incalculable. They are completely incalculable in earthly terms, as there is nothing on earth that would be sufficient to buy a single one of these gifts. There is only one calculation for the price of these gifts—the life of the Son of God. No angel, no heavenly dominion, no saint could forgive you, free you, renew you, and sign your eternal adoption papers into the family of the Triune God. Christ alone has the authority, the power, and the desire to save you, and he paid every cost because he cares for you.

Week Five

BIBLE STUDY

READING & REFLECTION

Read 1 Peter 5:6-7

Intro Question: What do our anxieties reveal about where our hearts look for assurance and worth?

Read Psalm 22:1-18

1. How does this describe Christ's physical sufferings?

2. How does this describe Christ's emotional sufferings?

3. What confidence in our salvation do we gain by the specificity of these prophecies?

4. How does this describe the relationship between Christ and the Father on the Cross?

Read Isaiah 53

5. What specific prophecies does this passage make?

6. How do verses 6 & 10 help us understand our

salvation better?

7. How do verses 11 & 12 help us understand Christ as our brother better?

Read Matthew 27:27-57

8. Which prophecies did you notice from our previous passages that were fulfilled here?

9. How does this passage give evidence of Christ's love for us?

10. How do we know that Christ's sacrifice was acceptable to God for our redemption?

11. How does this passage affirm that there is only one means of salvation? (As opposed to multiple ways to get to God)

CHALLENGE

In what ways can we imitate the angels and look more deeply at the gospel of our salvation? What practical steps can we take to grow in appreciation for all that Christ has done, and how can we use that knowledge when we are anxious?